The Family of Woman

The Family of Woman

A Ridge Press Book Grosset & Dunlap New York

Editor and Publisher: **Jerry Mason**

Art Director: **Albert Squillace**

Project Editor: **Julia Scully**

Quotations Edited by Sylvia Cole

Editor: Adolph Suehsdorf
Associate Publisher: Ruth Birnkrant
Associate Editor: Ronne Peltzman
Associate Editor: Marta Hallett
Art Associate: Nancy Mack
Art Associate: Liney Li
Art Production: Doris Mullane

Assistant Project Editor: Mary O'Grady

The Family of Woman

Acknowledgments

Anonymous, from "Expatriate Rejects Autumn in New York" by Anatole Broyard. Copyright © 1977 by The New York Times Company. Reprinted by permission.

Yehuda Amichai, "A Pity. We Were Such A Good Invention," *Selected Poems,* translated by Assia Gutman, published 1971 by Penguin (U.K.). Copyright © 1968 by Cape Goliard. Reprinted by permission.

Karin Boye, "Yes It Hurts," translated from Swedish by May Swenson in *Half Sun Half Sleep,* published by Charles Scribner's Sons. Copyright © 1967 by May Swenson. Reprinted by permission of May Swenson.

Emily Dickinson. Reprinted by permission of the publishers and the Trustees of Amherst College from *The Poems of Emily Dickinson,* edited by Thomas H. Johnson, Cambridge, Mass.: The Belknap Press of Harvard University Press, Copyright © 1951, 1955 by the President and Fellows of Harvard College.

Henrik Ibsen, "A Doll's House," *Six Plays by Henrik Ibsen,* translated by Eva Le Gallienne, Copyright © 1961 by Eva Le Gallienne. Reprinted by permission of Random House.

Randall Jarrell, "The Night Before The Night Before Christmas," *The Complete Poems of Randall Jarrell.* Copyright © 1952 by Farrar, Straus & Giroux. Reprinted by permission.

Denise Levertov, from "Stepping Westward," *The Sorrow Dance.* Copyright © 1966 by Denise Levertov. Reprinted by permission of New Directions.

Eve Merriam, "Hey Money Money O," from *The Double Bed,* Copyright © 1958, 1972 by Eve Merriam. Reprinted by permission of the publisher, M. Evans and Company, Inc., New York, NY 10017.

Edna St. Vincent Millay, "Sonnet XLII," *Collected Poems,* Harper & Row. Copyright © 1928, 1955 by Edna St. Vincent Millay and Norma Millay Ellis.

Marianne Moore. Reprinted with permission of Macmillan Publishing Co., Inc., and Faber and Faber, Ltd., from "A Face," *Collected Poems of Marianne Moore.* Copyright © 1951 by Marianne Moore.

Edwin Muir, "The Refugees," from *Collected Poems.* Copyright © 1960 by Willa Muir. Reprinted by permission of Oxford University Press, Inc., and Faber and Faber, Ltd.

Ning Lao T'ai-t'ai, quoted by Ida Pruitt in *A Daughter of Han,* Stanford University Press, 1978. © 1945 Yale University Press. Reprinted by permission.

Boris Pasternak, from *Unpublished Letters of Boris Pasternak,* edited and translated by Elliot Mossman Copyright © 1977 by The New York Times Company. Reprinted by permission.

Pawnee poem, "Is This Real," excerpted from *In the Trail of the Wind,* edited by John Bierhorst. Copyright © 1971 by John Bierhorst. Reprinted with the permission of Farrar, Straus & Giroux, Inc.

Rachel: Page 19, from "My Dear," and page 146, from "My Strength Grows Less and Less," translated Robert Friend, *Anthology of Modern Hebrew Poetry,* Institute for the Translation of Hebrew Literature. Copyright © 1966 by Rachel.

Rainer Maria Rilke, *Letters to A Young Poet,* translated by M. D. Herter Norton. Used with the permissic of W. W. Norton & Company, Inc., and The Hogarth Press, Ltd. Copyright © 1934 by W. W. Norton & Company, Inc. Renewed 1962 by M. D. Herter Norton. Revised Edition Copyright © 1954 by W. W. Nor & Company, Inc.

Edith Sitwell, "The Canticle of the Rose." Reprinted from *The Collected Poems of Edith Sitwell* by permission of the Vanguard Press, Inc., and Macmillan, Ltd. Copyright © 1968 by the Vanguard Press, Copyright © 1949, 1954, 1959, 1962, 1963 by Dame Edith Sitwell.

Christina Stead: Page 22, from *The Puzzleheaded Girl,* Holt, Rinehart & Winston, copyright © 1965, 196 1967 by Christina Stead; and page 105, from *Dark Places of the Heart,* Holt, Rinehart & Winston, copyri © 1966 by Christina Stead. Reprinted by permission of Joan Daves.

Marina Tsvetayeva, "Poem of the End I," from *Marina Tsvetayeva: Selected Poems,* translated from the Russian by Elaine Feinstein. Copyright © 1971 by Oxford University Press. Reprinted by permissio

Mark Twain, reprinted courtesy of Harper & Row.

Diane Wakoski, "Beauty," Part III of "A Poet Recognizing the Echo of the Voice," *Magellanic Clouds,* Bla Sparrow Press, 1970. Reprinted by permission.

Elinor Wylie, "This Hand," *Collected Poems of Elinor Wylie.* Copyright © 1932 by Alfred A. Knopf, Inc., 1960 by Edwina C. Rubenstein. Reprinted by permission.

William Butler Yeats: Page 125, "Folly of Being Comforted," and page 169, "When You Are Old," reprint with permission of Macmillan Publishing Co., Inc., and A. P. Watt, Ltd., from *Collected Poems of William Butler Yeats.* Copyright © 1906 by Macmillan Publishing Co., Inc., renewed 1934 by William Butler Yea

THE FAMILY OF WOMAN—in the spirit of
THE FAMILY OF MAN and THE FAMILY OF CHILDREN.
From the world's photographers, a piercing look at the
changing and the unchanging, at universal woman and her progress
through life. THE FAMILY OF WOMAN looks at work, at activism, at play,
at sexual exploitation, at grief and death, at love. It looks at how
women feel and act with lovers, friends, parents,
husbands, children. Women's lives and the quality of womanhood:
THE FAMILY OF WOMAN illumines the changes that are
occurring within the great calm center
of what continues unchanged.

There is no savor
more sweet, more salt

Than to be glad to be
what, woman.

and who, myself
I am

Denise Levertov

U.S.A. Bill Binzen

The position of women in a society provides an exact measure of the development of that society.   Gustav Geiger

KENYA Jean-Jacques Dicker

JAPAN Elliott Erwitt/Magnu

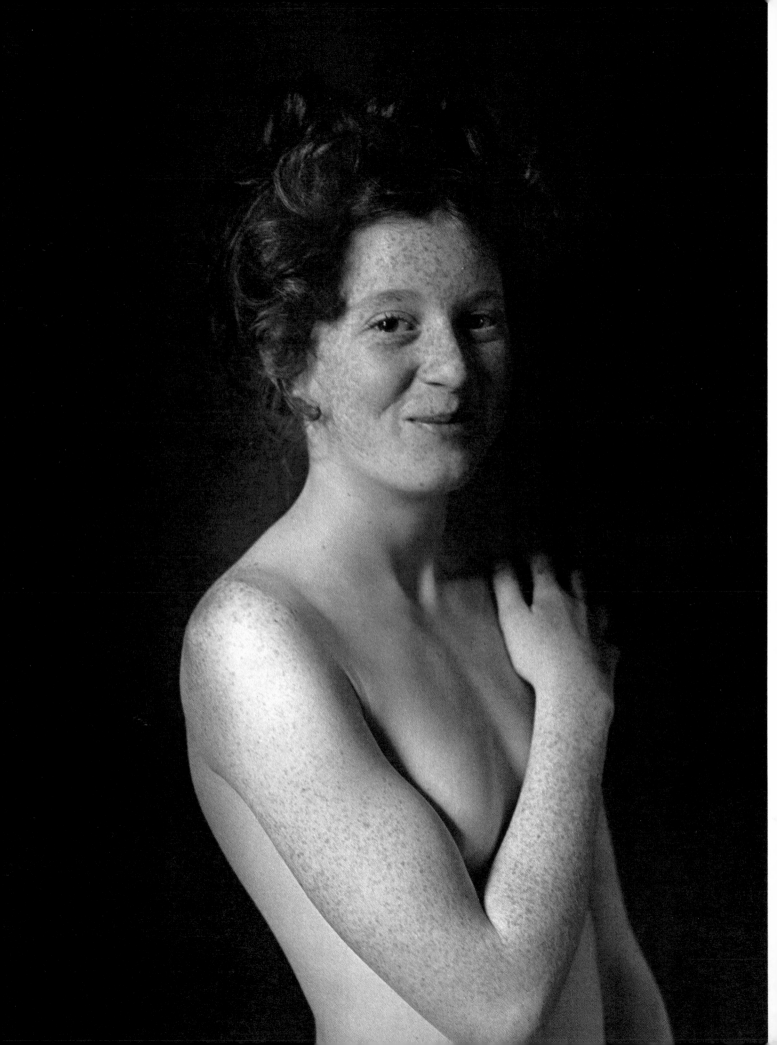

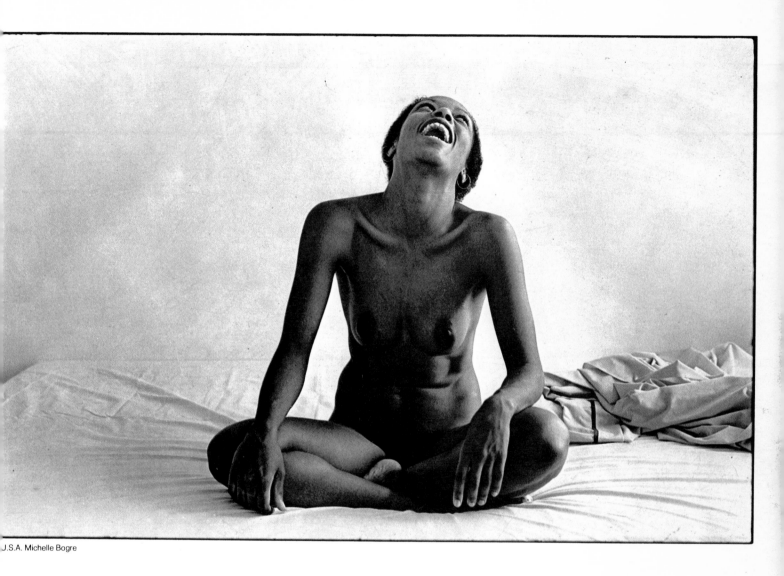

U.S.A. Michelle Bogre

When they gaze into my eyes, they see the truth.

NGLAND Bob Willoughby

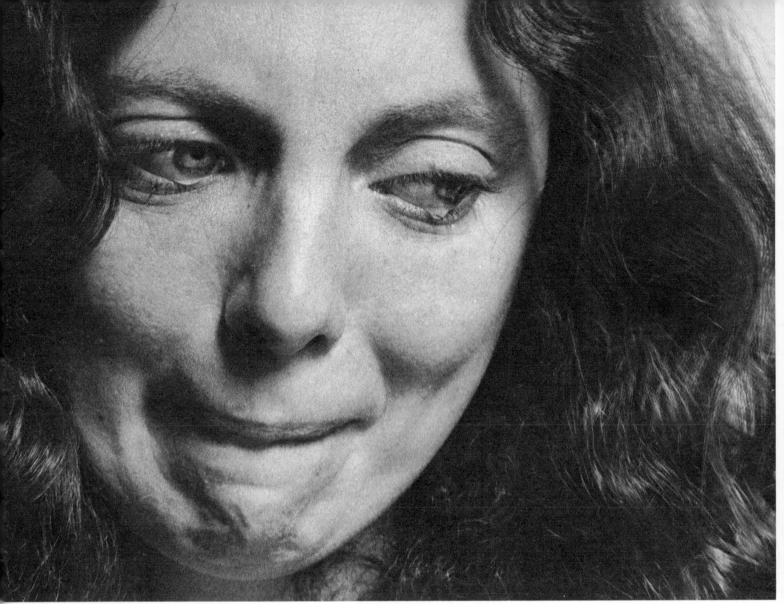

U.S.A. Zeva Oelbaum

I have
Immortal longings in me. Shakespeare

U.S.A. Sidney Kerner

15

U.S.A. Wayne Miller/Magnum

Yes it hurts when buds burst.

there is pain when something grows. Karin Boye

NORTHERN IRELAND Mary Ellen Mark/Magnu

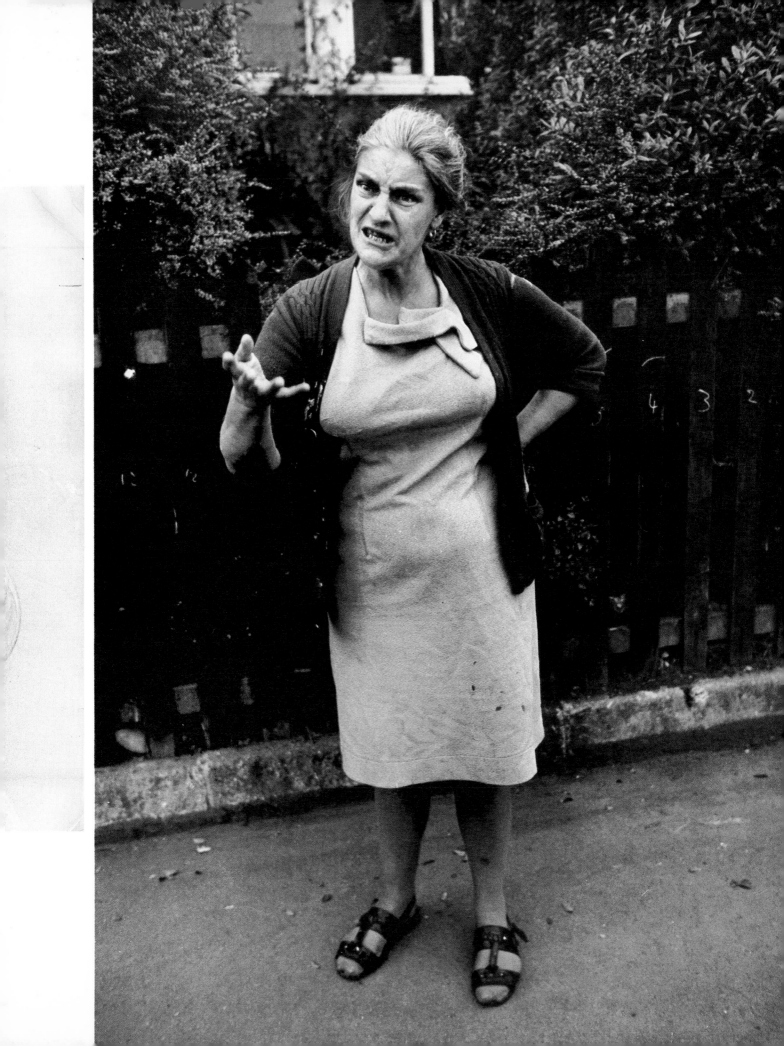

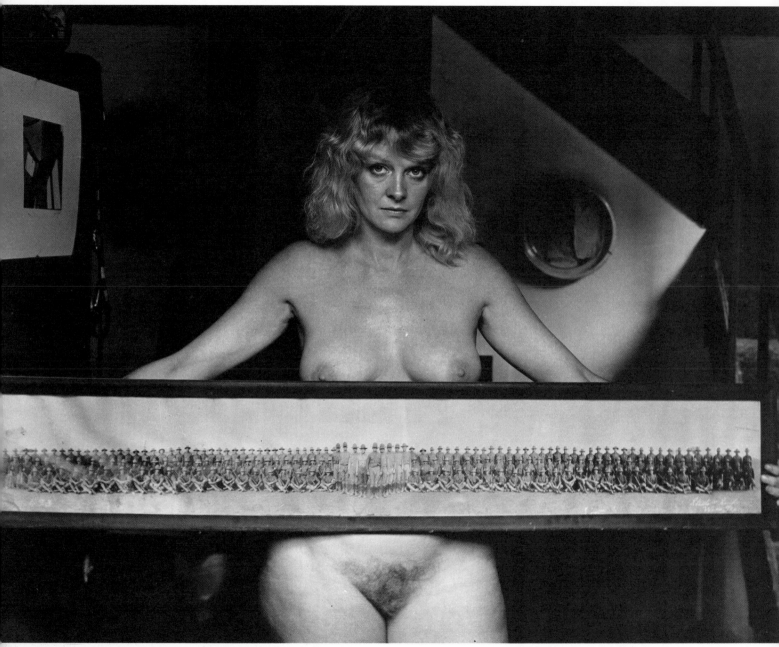

U.S.A. Judy Dater

U.S.A. Martin Munkacsi

Only what I have lost is what I possess forever. Rachel

IRELAND Evelyn Hofer

She thinks: What do I *really* look like?
I don't know.

Not really.
       Really.

Randall Jarrell

U.S.A. Frances McLaughlin-Gill

A woman can't be, until a girl dies. . . .
I mean the sprites that girls are, so different from us, all their
fancies, their illusions, their flower world, the
dreams they live in. Christina Stead

U.S.A. Beth Shepherd

FRANCE Esaias Baitel/Viva

VENEZUELA Bob Willoughby

NIGERIA Peter Martens/Nancy Palmer

NIGERIA Mary Ellen Mark/Magnum

24

EECE Stern/Black Star

U.S.A. Sheila Metzner/Daniel Wolf Gallery

U.S.A. George W. Gardner

U.S.A. Charles Harbutt/Magnum

U.S.A. Roger Malloch/Magnum

U.S.A. Bob Willoughby

She is femininity itself, extracted whole from the quarry of creation. Boris Pasternak

U.S.A. Frances McLaughlir

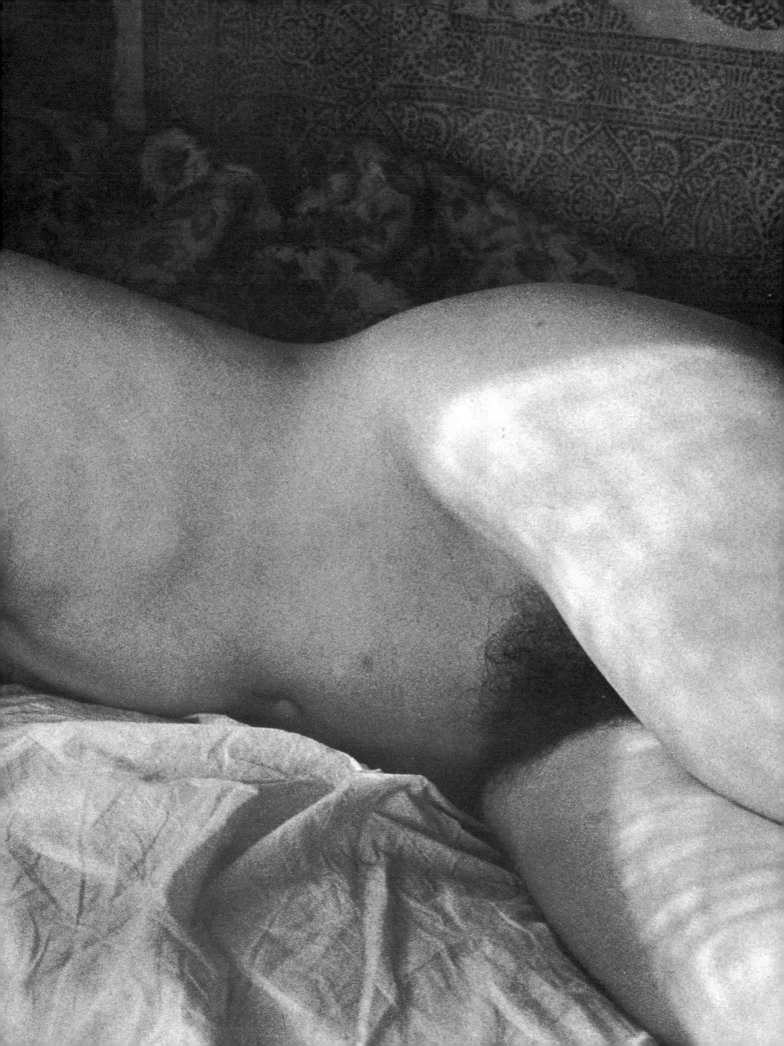

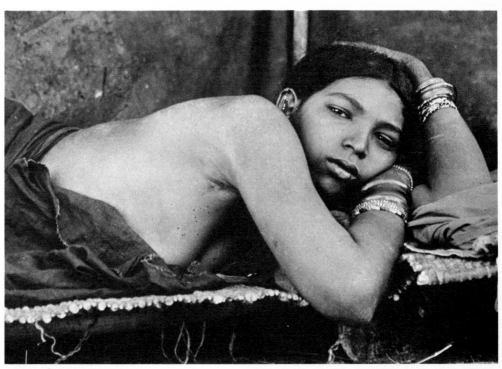

NIGER Victor Englebert/Leo de Wys Inc.

FRANCE Mary Ellen Mark/Magnum

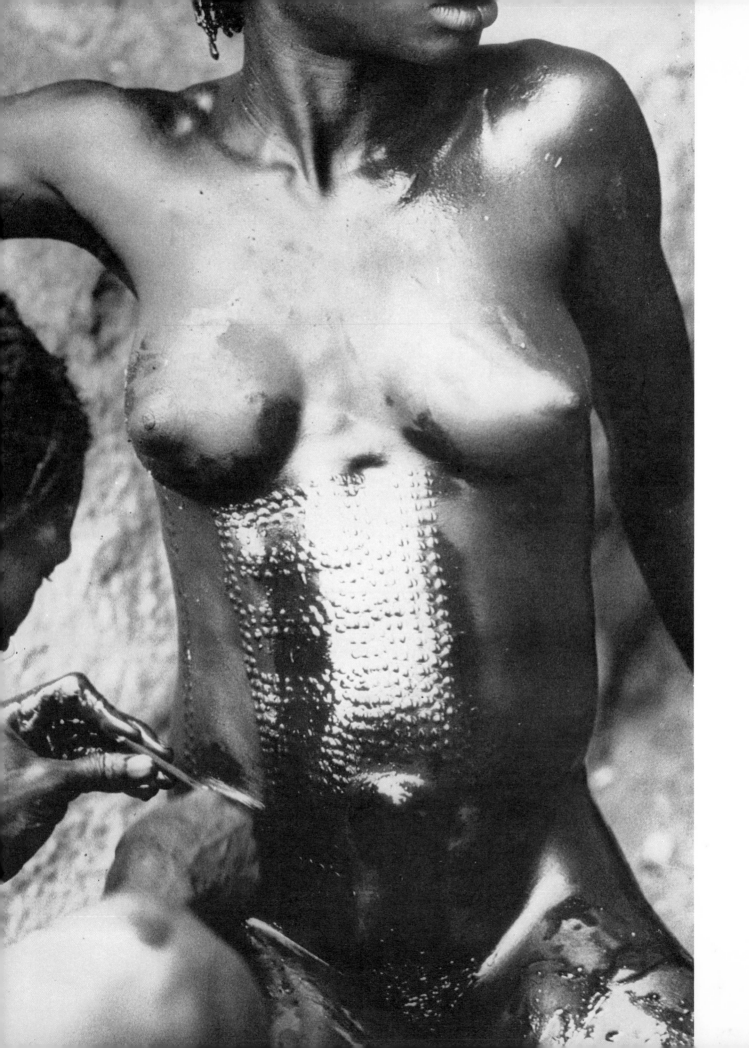

There is no excellent beauty that hath not some
strangeness in the proportion. Francis Bacon

FRANCE Eugène Atget/Museum of Modern Art

RAN Claudine Laabs

U.S.A. Charlotte March/FPG

SUDAN Leni Riefenstahl

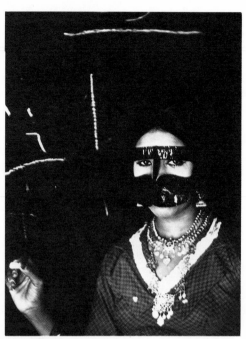

ABU DHABI Eve Arnold/Magnum

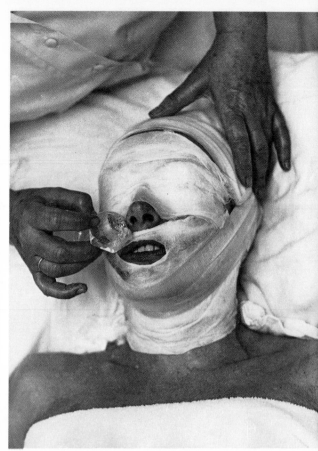

U.S.A. Eve Arnold/Magnum

U.S.A. Jay B. Mather

There is no torture that a woman would not endure to enhance her beauty. Montaigne

GER Marc Riboud/Magnum

NG KONG Ajong/New York Public Library

INDIA Edward Boubat/Rapho-Top

UGANDA Sven Gillsäter/Tio

U.S.A. Dick Swift

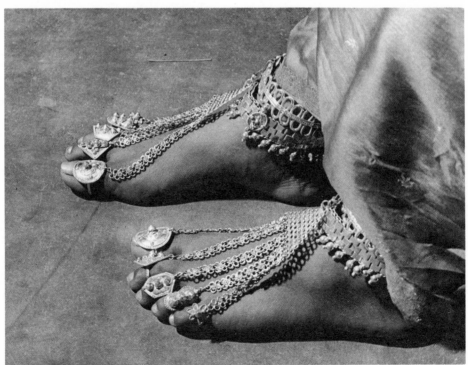

INDIA T. S. Satyan/Black Star

U.S.A. Dorothea Lange/Magn

FRANCE Alex Chatelain/Photo Trends

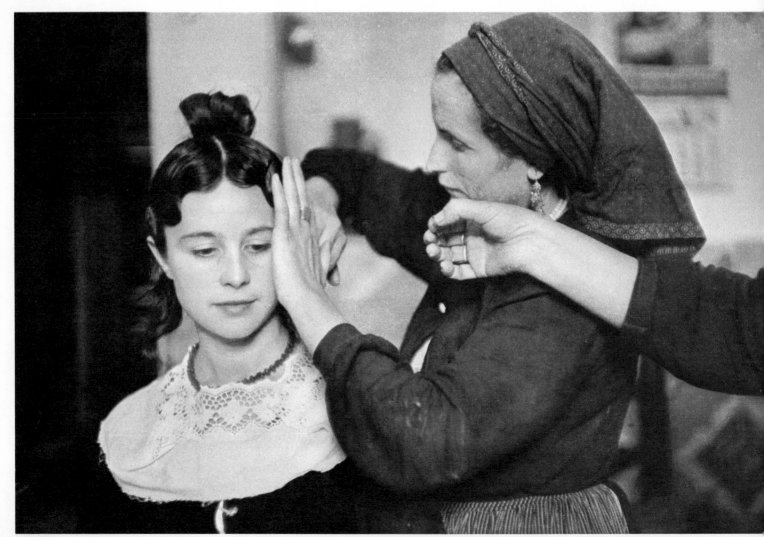

SPAIN Inge Morath/Magnum

TAHITI Dominique Darbois

U.S.A. A. C. Vroman/Los Angeles County Museum

U.S.A. Bill Owen/Magnum

U.S.A. Jack Manning/NYT Pictures

U.S.A. Michelle Bogre

Is there anywhere
a man
who
will not punish us
for our beauty?   Diane Wakoski

WALES Michelle Bogre

ENGLAND Pictorial Parade

U.S.A. Monte H. Gerlach

MEXICO Rudi Herzog

U.S.A. Gordon Munro

U.S.A. Charles Harbutt/Magnum

U.S.A. Shelly Rusten

Why, this is hell, nor am I out of it. Christopher Marlowe

© A. Roswell Angier

FRANCE Guy Le Querrec/Magnum

U.S.A. Sonia Moskowitz

U.S.A. Pam Spaulding/Courier-Journal & Louisville Times

VIETNAM Phillip James Griffiths/Magnum

INDIA J.P. Laffont/Sygma

THAILAND Stern/Black Star

...in Famine Street,

There is nothing left but the heart to eat. Edith Sitwell

U.S.A. Leon Levinst

U.S.A. Arthur Tress

BELGIUM Luuk Huiskes

U.S.A. UPI

U.S.A. Jill Freedman/Magnum

This hand you have observed,
Impassive and detached,
With joints adroitly curved,
And fingers neatly matched:

It doubles to a fist. Elinor Wylie

U.S.A. Louis Stettne

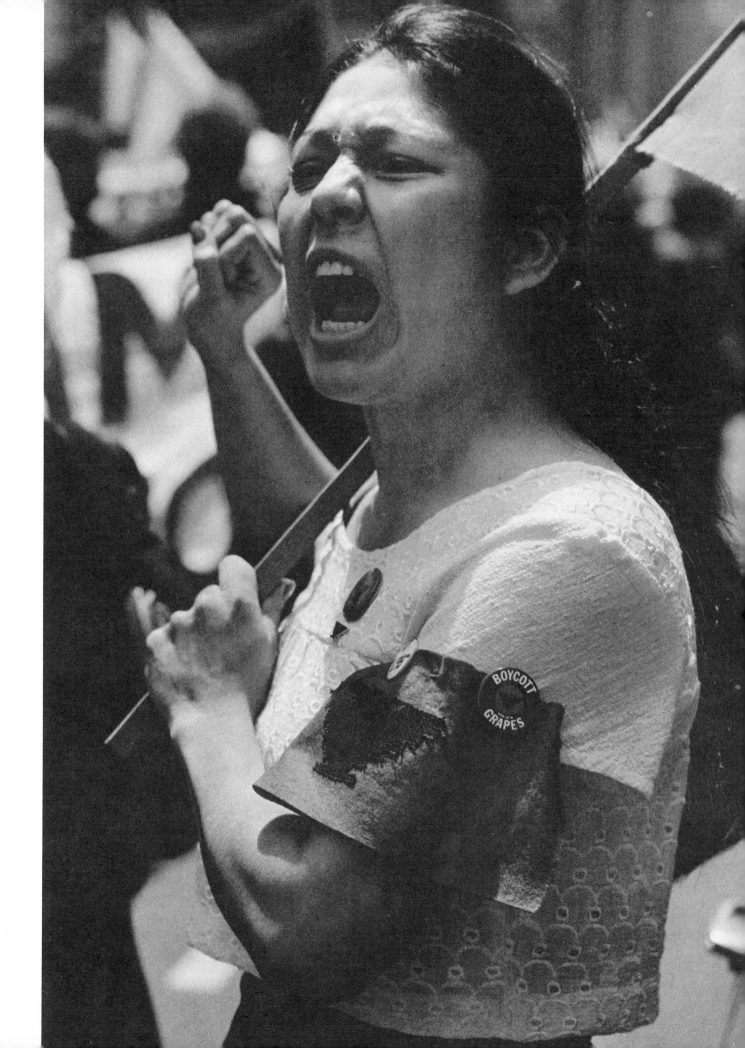

U.S.A. Bill Binzen

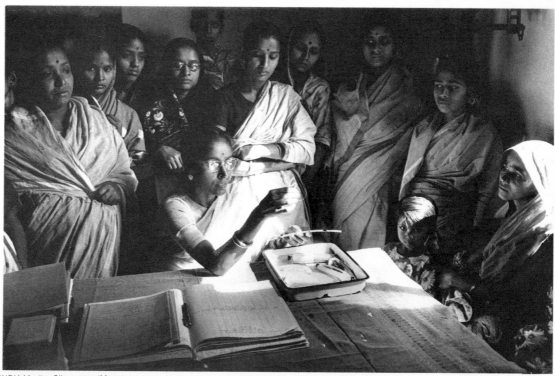

RU Ken Heyman

INDIA Marilyn Silverstone/Magnum

U.S.A. Bettye Lane

U.S.A. Ronald Wood/Black Star

WEST GERMANY Leonard Freed/Magnum

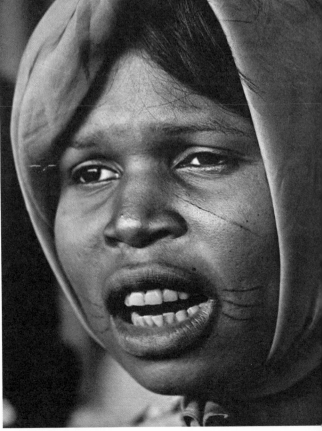

NIGERIA Marc and Evelyne Bernheim/Woodfin Camp

We must shape here a new philosophy. Edwin Muir

U.S.A. Leon Levir

ITALY Benjamin Hertzberg

CHINA Marc Riboud/Magnum

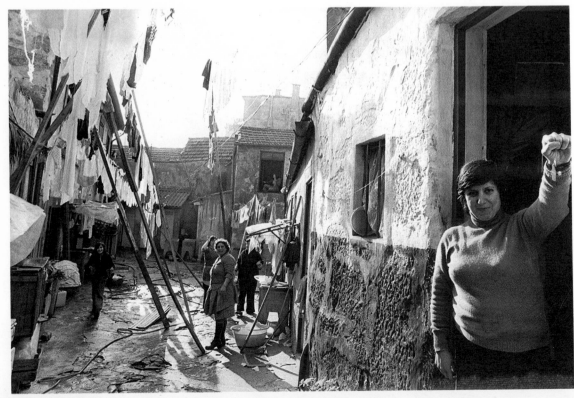

PORTUGAL Sylvan Julianne/Sygma

FRANCE Gilles Peress/Magnum

CHILE François Lehar

WEST GERMANY Thomas Höpker/Woodfin Camp

Her household motions light and free. William Wordsworth

GREECE Constantine Manos/Magnum

ANTIGUA Melchior DiGiacomo

INDIA Wolff/UNICEF

ENGLAND Homer Sykes/John Hillelson Agency

She looketh well to
the ways of her household, and
eateth not the bread of idleness. Proverbs 31:27

INDIA Bernard Pierre Wolff

BANGLADESH Heldur J. Netocny

but when we get to them we bear them. Ning Lao T'ai-t'ai

U.S.A. Jim Smith

HAWAII Jerry Gay

FRANCE Sabine Weiss/Photo Researchers

TIBET Mario Giacomelli

FRANCE Charlie Asad/Viva

ITALY Catherine Ursillo

Let us see, is this real,

Let us see, is this real,

This life I am living? Pawnee poem

INDIA Gianfranco Gorgoni/Leo de Wys Inc.

U.S.A. Bill Owen

74

U.S.A. Sardi Klein

U.S.A. James H. Barker

DENMARK Gregers Nielsen

FRANCE Marc Riboud/Magnum

U.S.A. Sepp Seitz/Woodfin Camp

Whatever women do they must do twice as well as men
to be thought half as good. Luckily, this is not difficult. Charlotte Whitton

U.S.A. Abigail Heyman/Magnum

U.S.A. Dick Frank

CHINA Richard and Sally Greenhill

U.S.A. Eve Arnold/Magnum

MEXICO Filip Tas

Women feel just as men feel...and it is narrow-minded in their more privileged fellow-creatur

NEW ZEALAND Ross G. Giblin

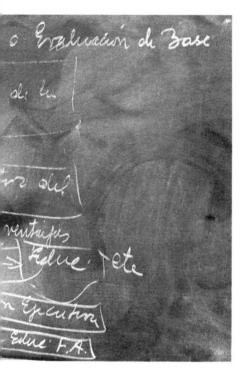

U.S.A. Alex Traube

say that they ought to confine themselves to making puddings and knitting stockings. Charlotte Brontë

81

ITALY F. Harlan Hambright

My true love hath my heart, and I have his. Sir Philip Sidney

U.S.A. Shelly Rusten/Black Star

MEXICO Leon Levinstein

FRANCE Bogdan Paluszynski

But this dark is deep:

now I warm you with my blood, listen

to this flesh.

It is far truer than poems.   Marina Tsvetayeva

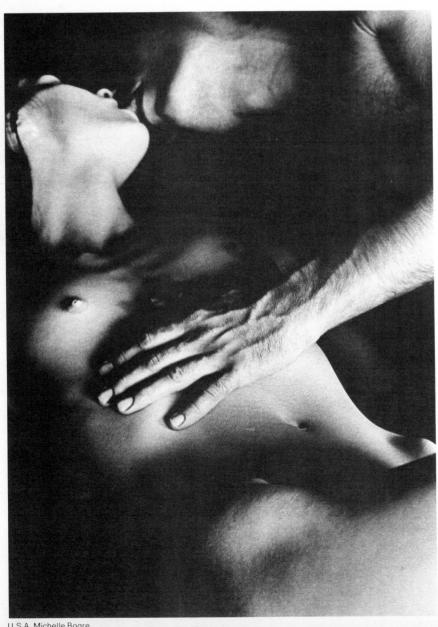

U.S.A. Michelle Bogre

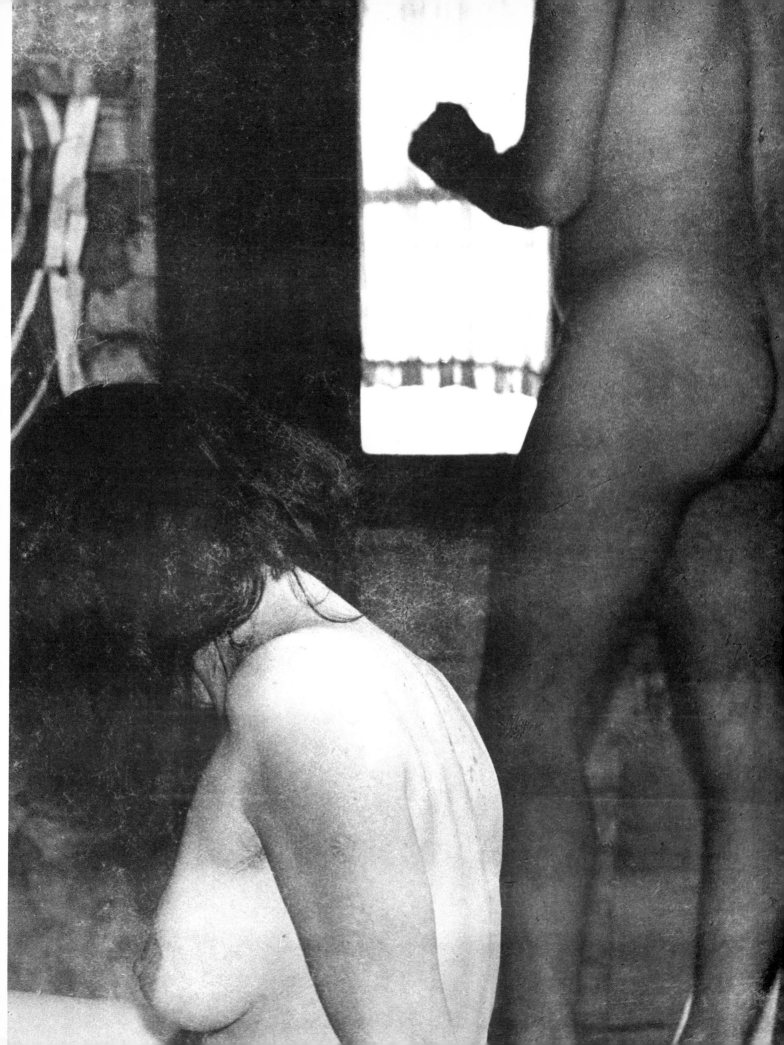

U.S.A. Eugene Richards/Magnum

Preceding pages: U.S.A. Charles Harbutt/Magnum

JAPAN Hiroji Kubota

I never perform the marriage ceremony without a renewed sense of the iniquity of a system by which man and wife are one, and that one is the husband.   Thomas Higginson

U.S.A. Nancy Moran

Sylvia Plachy

91

U.S.A. Sardi Klein

LATVIA V. Brauns/Sovfoto

PUERTO RICO Harold Goldbaum

For one human being to love another: that is perhaps
the most difficult of all our tasks, the ultimate,
the last test and proof, the work for which all other
work is but preparation.   Rainer Maria Rilke

©A. Bruce Gilden

95

U.S.A. Catherine Ursillo

U.S.A. Disfarmer, U.S.A.

MEXICO Susan Shapiro

U.S.A. Eugene Richards/Magnum

ISRAEL Sherry Suris

WEST GERMANY Thomas Höpker/Woodfin Camp

SWEDEN Nils-Johan Norenlind/Tio

U.S.S.R. Eve Arnold/Magnum

WEST GERMANY Leonard Freed/Magnum

…We were such a good
And loving invention.
An aeroplane made from a man and wife.
Wings and everything.
We hovered a little above the earth.

We even flew a little. Yehuda Amichai

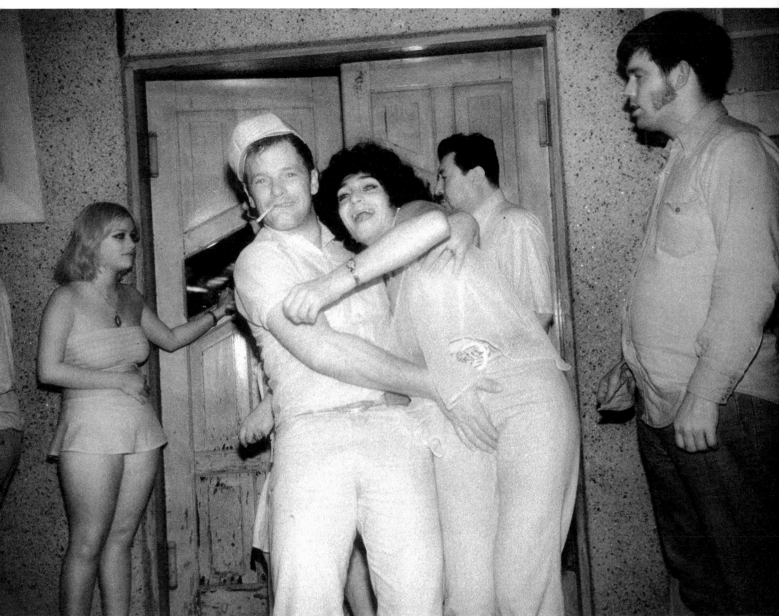

MEXICO Alex Webb/Magnum

U.S.A. Joan Liftin/Woodfin Camp

MEXICO Alex Webb/Magnum

GREECE Michael Semak

102

EAST GERMANY Thomas Höpker/Woodfin Camp

FRANCE Jean-Philippe Charbonnier

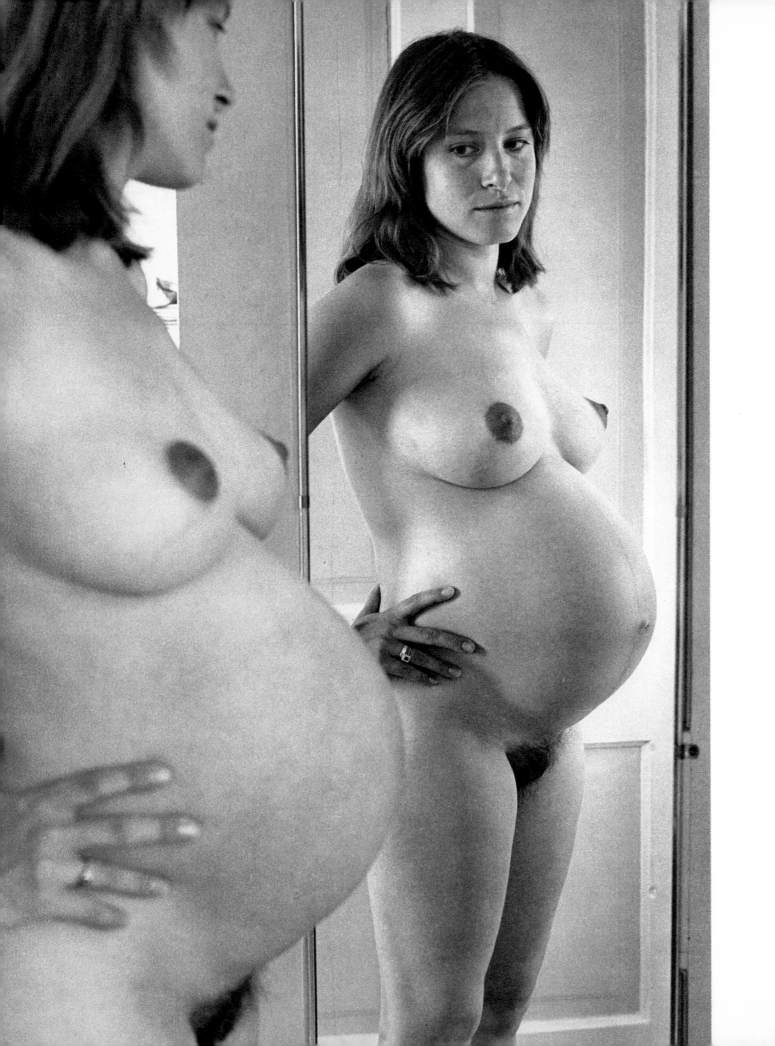

S.A. Robert D'Alessandro

A. Monte H. Gerlach

They were young things when they had us. ready for life
and we were the first burden on their thin young shoulders.
I don't understand those who don't feel this terrible
tender guilt towards their parents. Christina Stead

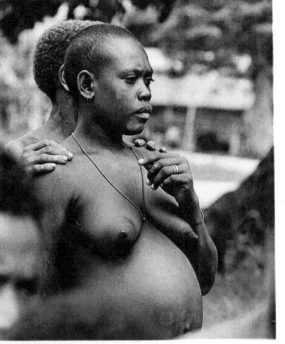

SOLOMON ISLANDS Jörgen Lundberg/Tio

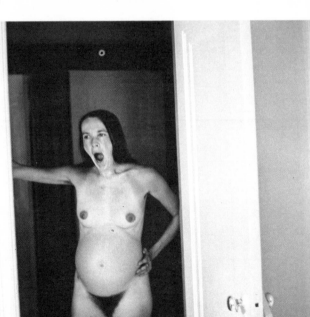

WEST GERMANY Stern/Black Star

U.S.A. Anthony Wolff

U.S.A. Bernis von zur Muehlen

.A. Joanne Leonard/Woodfin Camp

FRANCE Richard Kalvar/Magnum

_AND Bryn Campbell/John Hillelson Agency

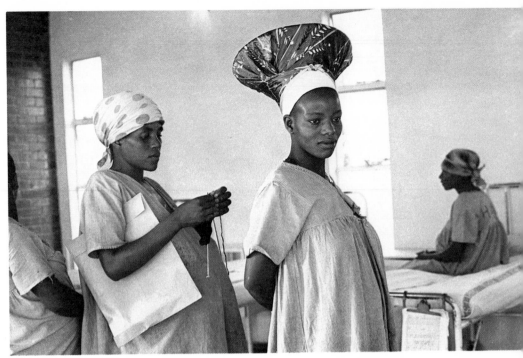

SOUTH AFRICA Eve Arnold/Magnum

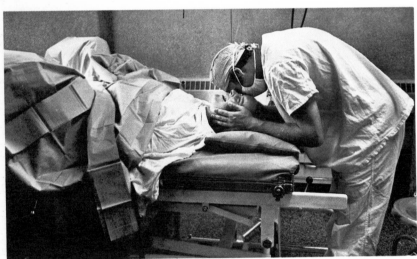

U.S.A. Abigail Heyman/Magnum

U.S.A. Mariette Pathy Allen

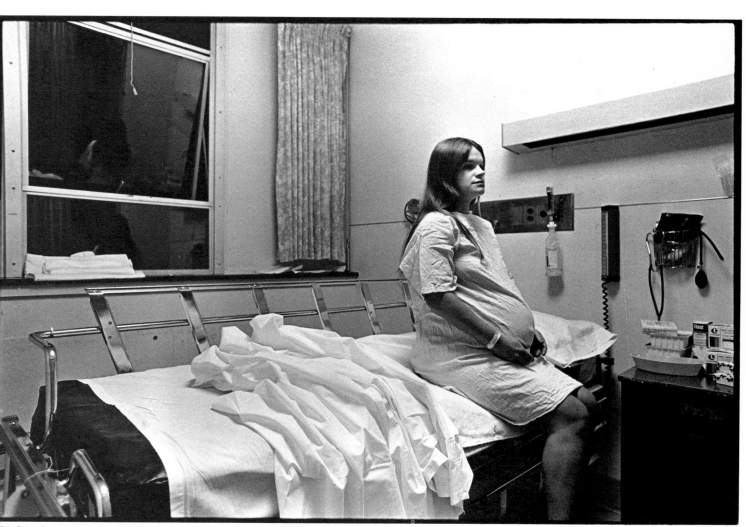

S.A. Gabor Demien/Stock. Boston

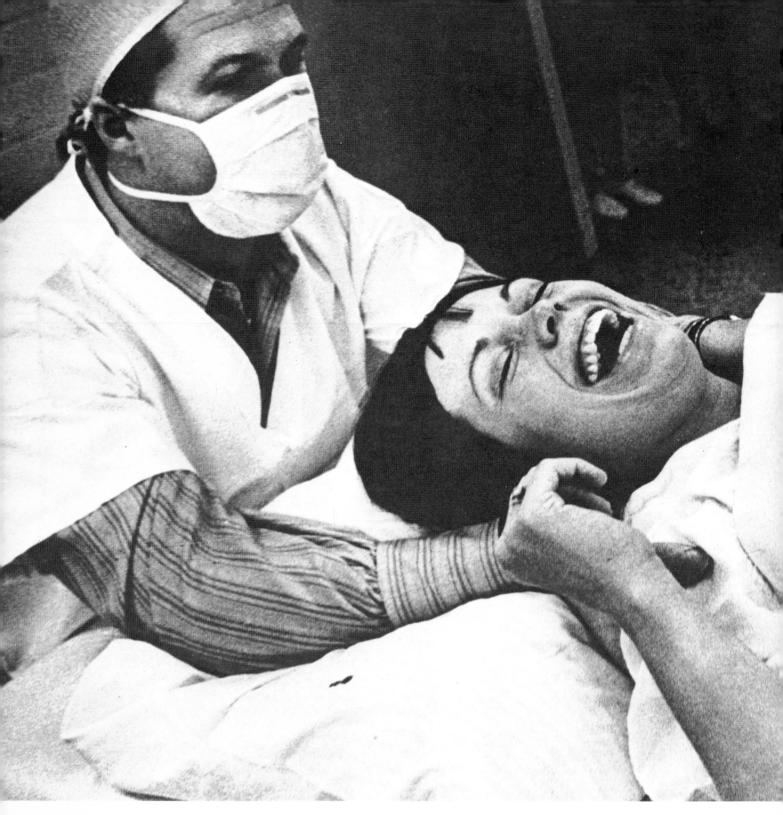

U.S.A. Brian Lanker

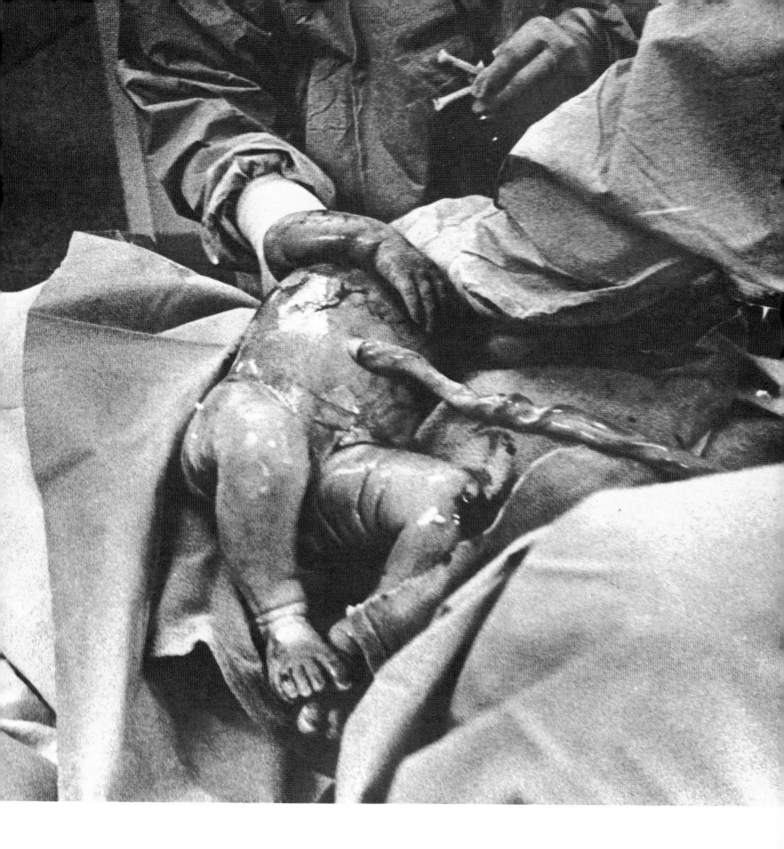

U.S.A. Alison E. Wachstein

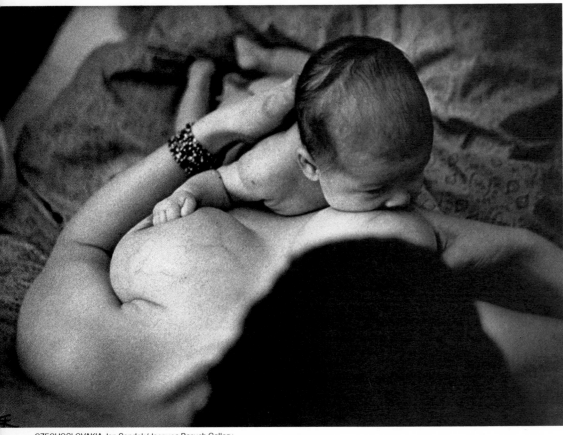

CZECHOSLOVAKIA Jan Sandek / Jacques Baruch Gallery

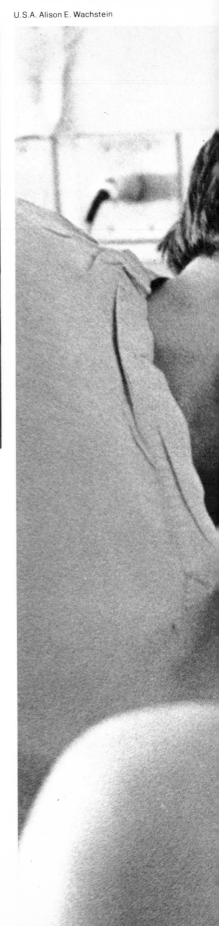

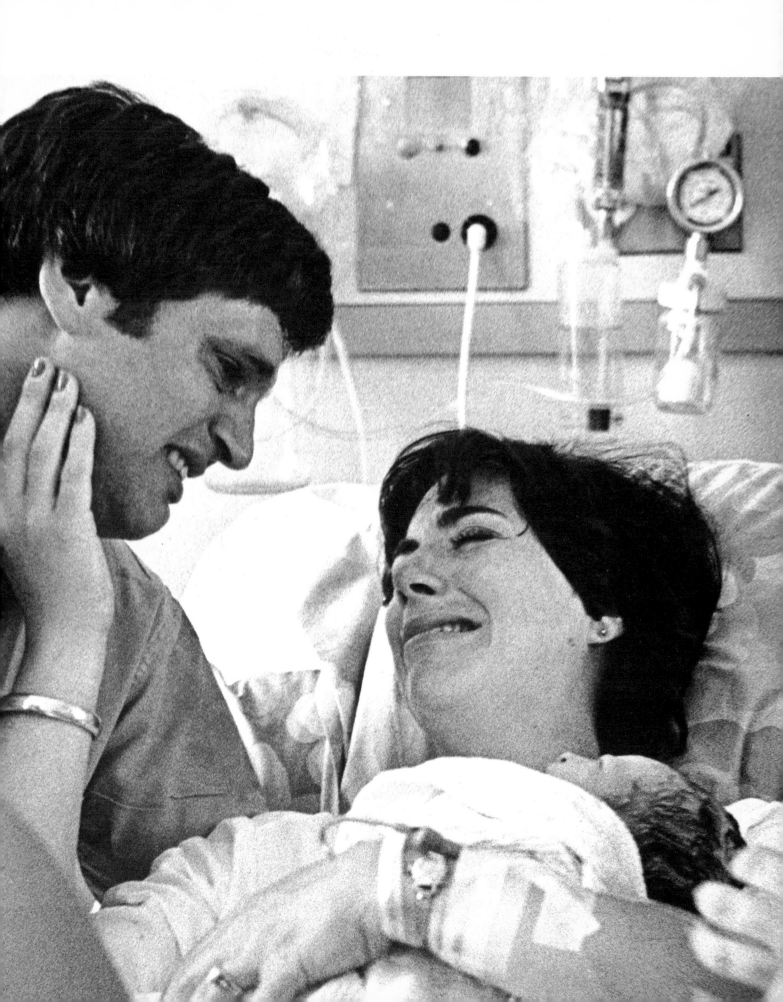

They would be scarce, sir, almighty scarce. Mark Twain

U.S.A. Dick Swift

U.S.A. Maura McCaw

U.S.A. Sepp Seitz/Woodfin Camp

GHANA Michael Semak

NEPAL Elaine Brière

U.S.A. Catherine Noren

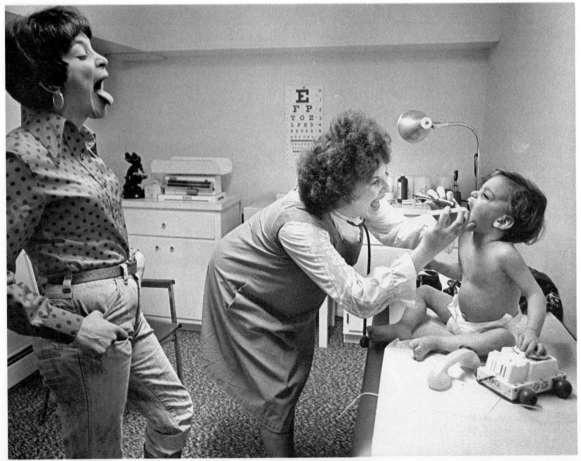

U.S.A. Alison E. Wachstein

U.S.A. Susan Meiselas/Magnum

SENEGAL Alain Noques/Sygma

U.S.A. Dick Frank

All are needed by each one;

Nothing is fair or good alone. Ralph Waldo Emerson

GREECE Constantine Manos/Magnum

U.S.A. Sherry Suris

U.S.A. Leonard Freed/Magnum

FRANCE Richard Kalvar/Magnum

ENGLAND Ian Berry/Magnum

U.S.A. Melissa K. Farlou/Courier-Journal & Louisville Times

FRANCE Guy Le Querrec/Magnum

U.S.A. Joanne Leonard/Woodfin Camp

U.S.A. Abigail Heyman/Magnum

124

INDIA Mary Ellen Mark/Magnum

WALES Alana Michael

My mother dandled me and sang,

"How young it is, how young!" William Butler Yeats

ZAIRE Sonia Katchian

IRAN Stern/Black Star

U.S.A. Alma Davenport

U.S.A. Nancy Rudolph

A. Catherine Ursillo

WALES UPI

U.S.A. Eugene Richards/Magnum

U.S.A. Elizabeth Hamlin/Stock, Boston

Thou art thy mother's glass. and she in thee
Calls back the lovely April of her prime. Shakespeare

U.S.A. Arthur Tress

WEST GERMANY Thomas Höpker/Woodfin Camp

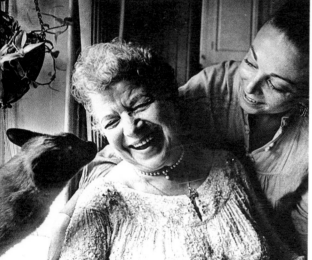

U.S.A. Joel Gordon/DPI

U.S.A. Abigail Heyman/Magnum

U.S.A. Aliza Auerbach

Mine, O thou lord of life, send my roots rain. Gerard Manley Hopkins

PUERTO RICO Marc and Evelyne Bernheim/Woodfin Camp

The Rosary is recited here every Sunday at 3.30 & 6.00 for World Peace and every need.

It is led by the 'Blue Army' of our Lady, a worldwide organisation of 20,000,000 members, who, by offering themselves to God have pledged to work for World Peace by prayer and the penance of their daily work.

We believe that prayer is the only effective way of obtaining that peace which the world desires and so badly needs.

The Blue Army was formed to fulfil requests made by Mary the Mother of Jesus Christ at Fatima Portugal 1917.

ENGLAND Monte H. Gerlach

MEXICO Lazaro Blanco

134   CZECHOSLOVAKIA Martin Martinček

ALY Santo Piano

U.S.A. Milton Rogovin

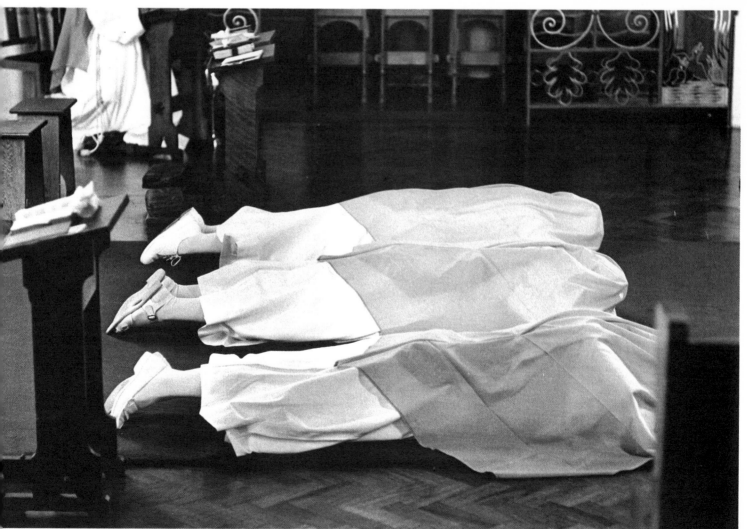

GLAND Eve Arnold/Magnum

ENGLAND Homer Sykes/John Hillelson Agency

That thrilling free feeling of feeling free wheeling. Eve Merriam

U.S.A. John Avery

U.S.A. Jim Mendelhall

U.S.A. Bettye Lane

S.A. David Carl Trunley

U.S.A. Warren Morgan

A. Lucinda W. Bunnen

U.S.A. Joan Liftin/Woodfin Camp

U.S.A. Dena

U.S.S.R. G. German/Sovfoto

FRANCE Gilles Peress/Magnum

Woman is woman's natural ally. Euripides

U.S.A. Eugene Richards/Magnum

Be my heart's prop.

In the waste places be a shade-giving tree.

Be good to me!

The night is long, the dawn is far away.

Be a small light, be a sudden joy,

be my daily bread. Rachel

S.A. Richard Kalvar/Magnum

U.S.A. Suzanne Szasz

The ladies looked one another over with microscopic carelessness. Arthur "Bugs" Baer

U.S.A. Richard Kalvar/Magnum

U.S.A. Garry Winogrand

ISRAEL F. B. Grunzweig

GREECE Bernard Pierre Wolff

152

WEST GERMANY Thomas Höpker/Woodfin Camp

IRELAND Brian Seed/John Hillelson Agency

APAN George Bellerose/Stock, Boston

SPAIN Ken Heyman

ITALY Enzo Sellerio

Never am I less alone than when I am by myself, never am
I more active than when I do nothing. Cato

WEST GERMANY Henning Christoph

ENGLAND Richard and Sally Greenh

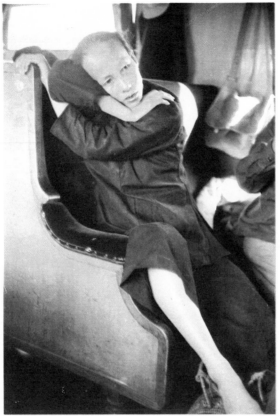

CHINA Marc Riboud/Magnum

U.S.A. Edward Miller

FRANCE Jill Freedman

U.S.A. Harry Lapow

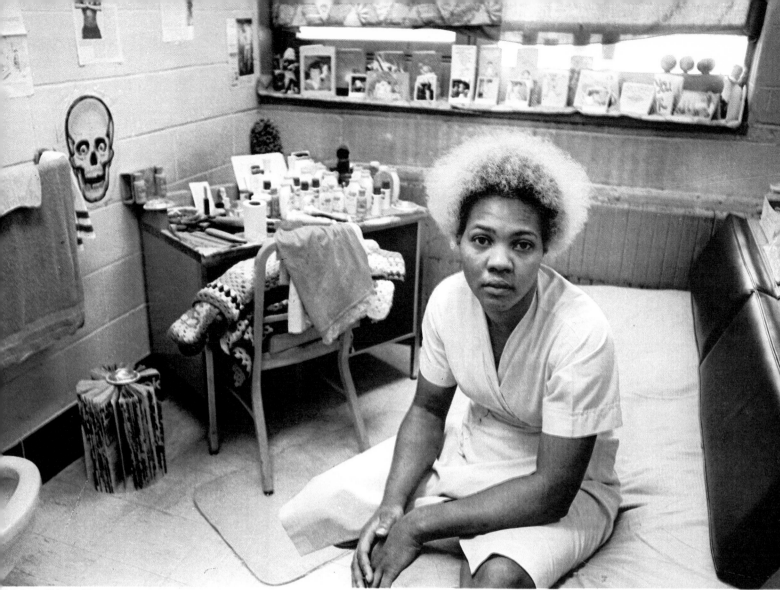

S.A. Susan Meiselas/Magnum

S.A. Monte H. Gerlach

ALGERIA Anders Cederholm

And in my heart there stirs a quiet pain
For unremembered lads that not again
Will turn to me at midnight with a cry. Edna St. Vincent Millay

U.S.A. Jim Smith

WEST GERMANY Bernard Pierre Wolff

Civilization begins at home.   Henry James

U.S.A. Kenneth Murray/Nancy Palmer

U.S.A. Will Faller

U.S.A. East Baltimore Documentary Photography Project

POLAND Joanna Helander

U.S.A. Sardi Klein

U.S.A. Elizabeth Hamlin/Stock, Boston

When you are old and grey and full of sleep,
And nodding by the fire . . .
. . . dream of the soft look
Your eyes had once, and of their shadows deep. William Butler Yeats

U.S.A. Abigail Heyman/Magnum

ENGLAND Bob Willoughby

JAPAN Ken Heyman

U.S.A. Abigail Heyman/Magnum

U.S.A. Ken Heyman

FRANCE Cary Wolinsky/Stock, Boston

I am my husband's life as fully as he is mine. Charlotte Brontë

ST GERMANY Thomas Höpker/Woodfin Camp

I am declined
Into the vale of years. Shakespeare

ITALY Mario Giacomelli

U.S.A. Randy Matusow

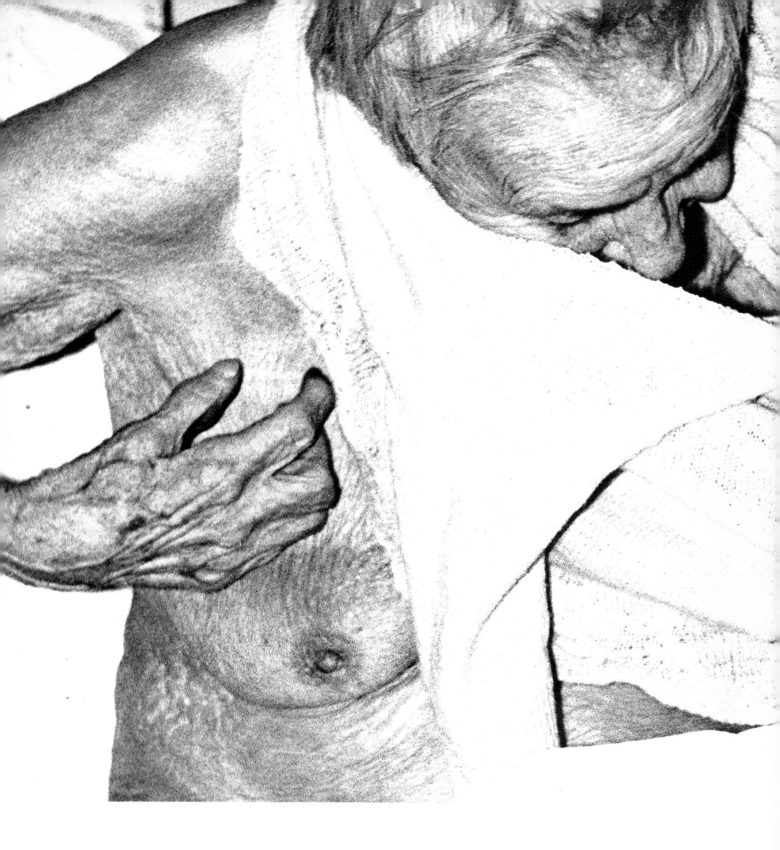

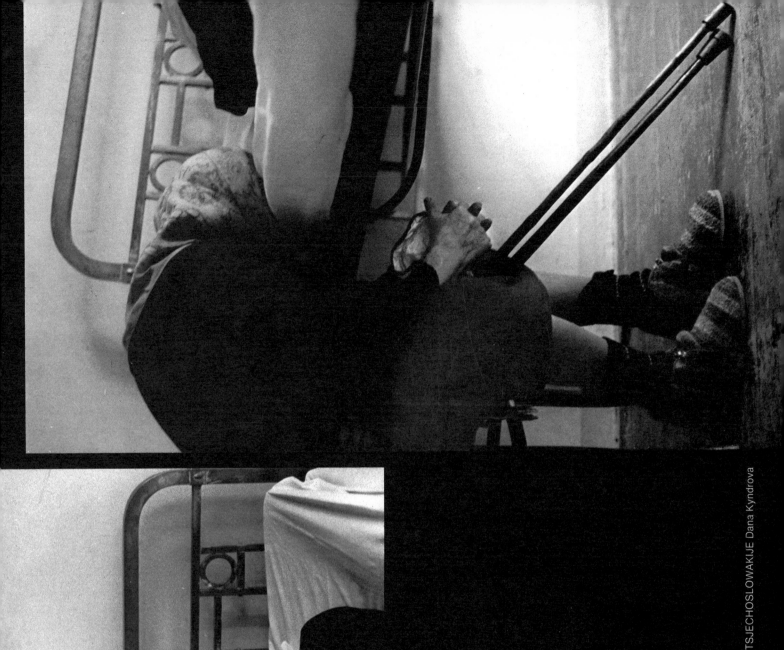

ITALY Mario Giacomelli

Because I could not stop for Death,

He kindly stopped for me. Emily Dickinson

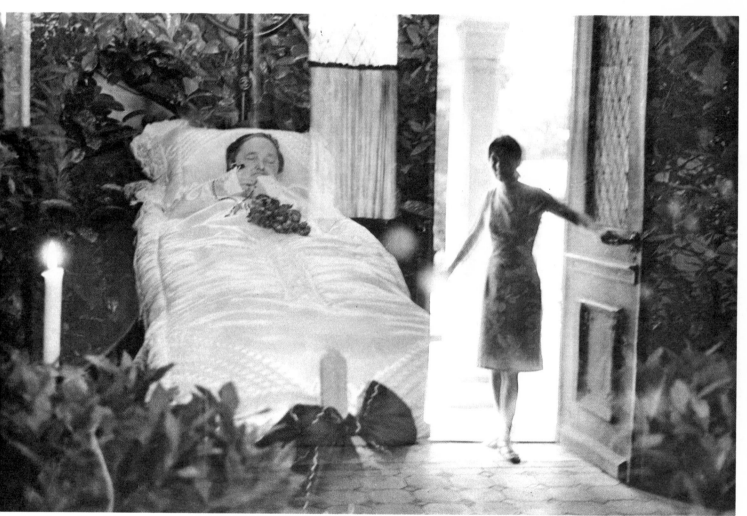

GERMANY Leonard Freed/Magnum

ENGLAND Julian Calder/Woodfin Camp

THE NETHERLANDS Brand M. Overeem

U.S.A. Michael O'Brien

GREECE Constantine Manos/Magnum

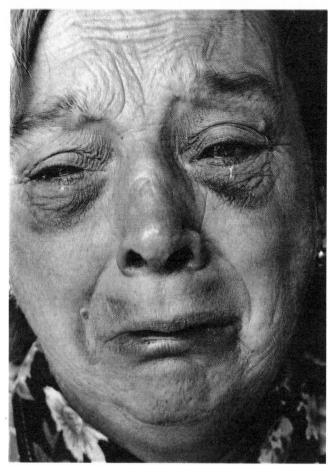

U.S.A. Eugene Richards/Magnum

U.S.A. Sepp Seitz/Woodfin Camp

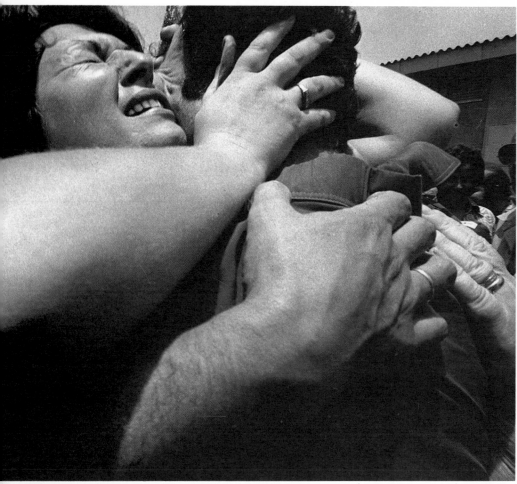

ISRAEL Micha Bar-Am/Magnum

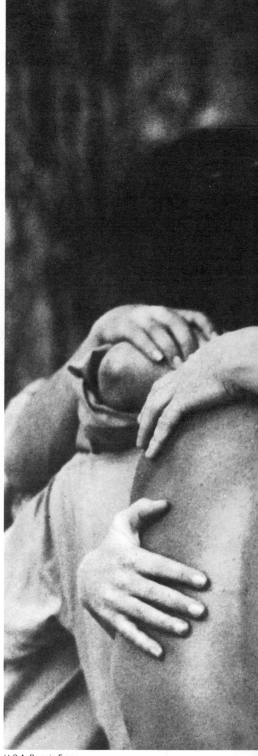

U.S.A. Bonnie Freer

Comforter, where, where is your comforting?   Gerard Manley Hopkins

U.S.A. Ken Heyman

I am giddy, expectation whirls me round. Shakespeare

GREECE Hanns-Jörg Anders

U.S.A. Nancy Moran

IVORY COAST Marc and Evelyn Bernheim/Woodfin Camp

U.S.A. Judy Dater

INDIA Thomas Höpker/Woodfin Camp

U.S.A. Jack Caspary/Woodfin Camp

Certain faces, a few, one or two—or one
face photographed by recollection—
     to my mind, to my sight,
     must remain a delight. Marianne Moore

U.S.A. Gary Goldberg

U.S.A. Anthony Barboza

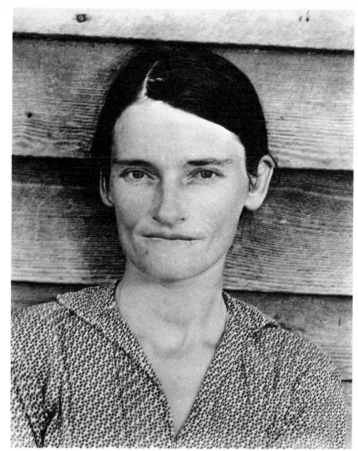

U.S.A. Walker Evans/Library of Congress

Richard Gordon

U.S.A. John Running/Black Star

U.S.A. Bill Binzen

HELMER: Remember—before all else you are a wife and mother.

NORA: I don't believe that anymore.

I believe that before all else I am a human being, just as you are. Henrik Ibsen